Small

Roger Elkin

Littoral Press

First published 2023 by
Littoral Press, 15 Harwood Place,
Lavenham, Sudbury, Suffolk CO10 9SG

ISBN 978-1-912412-47-1

British Library Cataloguing-in-Publication Data:
A catalogue record of this book is available from
The British Library

Printed and bound in Great Britain by
4Edge Ltd. Hockley, Essex
www.4edge.co.uk

Roger Elkin lives in the Staffordshire Moorlands. His poems have won **63** First Prizes in (inter)national Poetry Competitions; the *Sylvia Plath Award for Poems about Women*; and the *Howard Sergeant Memorial Award for Services to Poetry* (1987*)*.

He organized the Leek Arts Festival International Poetry Competition (1982-1992); was the co-Editor of *Prospice*, the international literary quarterly, (issues 17-25); Editor of *Envoi* 1991-2006, (issues 101-145); and poetry tutor at Wedgwood College, Barlaston.

He is available for reading, book-signings, poetry workshops and competition adjudication: contact eiger@hotmail.co.uk for details.

Other Publications:

Poetry

Pricking Out	(Aquila, 1988)
Points of Reference	(Headland, 1996)
Home Ground	(Headland, 2002)
Blood Brothers	(Headland, 2005)
Rites of Passing	(Shoestring, 2006)
No Laughing Matter	(Cinnamon Press, 2007)
Dog's Eye View	(Lapwing, 2009)
Fixing Things	(Indigo Dreams, 2011)
Bird in the Hand	(Indigo Dreams, 2012)
Marking Time	(Sentinel Poetry Movement, 2013)
Chance Meetings	(Poetry Space, 2014)
Sheer Poetry	(Dempsey & Windle, 2020)
The Leading Question	(The High Window, 2021)

Prose:

Critical articles on Ted Hughes's **Recklings** poems in collections of essays edited by Keith Sagar, **The Challenge of Ted Hughes**, (St.Martin's Press, [1995]); Joanny Moulin, **Lire Ted Hughes,** (Edition du Temps, [1999]); and on **The Ted Hughes Society** and **Earth-moon Ted Hughes** websites

Acknowledgements

are due to the editors of the various magazines and anthologies in which earlier versions of these poems appeared:

Another Nest of Singing Birds, Edward Thomas Fellowship Anthology (2019); **Barnet Open Anthology** (2013); Decanto; Envoi; *Eternal,* Hammond House Anthology (2017); **Green Spaces**; *Harvest,* An Anthology, Binsted Arts (2017); **origami poems and towering stories**; **Onward Writing Anthology**; Poetry Pulse; Poetry Space Autumn Showcase 2014; Salopeot; Savistrati; Sentinel Poetry Quarterly; The HighWindow; The Rosemary McLeish Poetry Prize Anthology (2021); The Ver Prize Anthology (2019); *The Water's Edge,* Yes Arts Festival Anthology (2017); *Write Path,* NAWG Anthology (2016)

The following poems have won prizes in (inter)national Open Competitions:

Beached Jellyfish	1st, Lord Whisky Sanctuary	2018
Cornflower	2nd, Poetry Space	2011
Fishy Triptych	1st, May OPC	2013
Hive	2nd, Samuel Coleridge Taylor Memorial	2009
Hyacinth	3rd, Barnet	2013
Me, My Mum & Great-crested Newt		
	1st, Poetry Pulse	2015
On A Wood Pigeon Proposition		
	1st, NAWG	2016
Paeony	2nd, Newark	2011
Remembering Sheelagh's Way		
	3rd, NAWG	2017
Small Fry	1st, NAWG	2013
White Phlox	1st, Tenby	2011

For Eileen, who has other fish to fry

CONTENTS

Paeony

Finger the orb of her bud,
firm with the firmness of shotty glass –
smooth, round – its green and white
flecked with maroon
like specks of dried blood,
so hard, so cold
you'd be forgiven for thinking
she's done for, well past her best.

Yet when days later she bursts into bloom,
flouncing fuller, fuller
like a big Mama in her best festival hat
she's such a blowsy dresser
that, sensing she's top-drawer,
she flaunts herself, clowning about
as if everything's gone to her head
and she's giving you the come-on.

It's then your fingers begin to linger
over her satin-thin skin
not that pink-silkiness of the newborn
not the virginal ermine white
but the red of the freshly-snecked wound –
shiny, certain – as if sporting a warning:

Handle me, yes.
Finger. Stroke. Pluck.
Even cut me.

But don't ever think
of moving me.

Don't

9

Hyacinth: resurrection forfeit

So Apollo took up the lad's body
in his arms where he lay, concussed,
dying from the thrown discuss blown
off-course by Zephyr vying for his love,
and cradling him caressed away the sweat
glistening his limbs and furling his locks –
golden, curled – then, cupping hand,
caught the lad's spilled blood and fashioned
it into flower, his grief staining the thin-skin
petals – *ai, ai* – with his tears.

This the resurrection: this cheating
of death via a rising: leaf-tip nippling
through, smooth stem pushing in a sheen
of gleam, a glans of bud lancing to thrust
upwards and break, headily, into bloom –
curled, curving – its heavy scent stealing
breath away and masking the fact that,
hidden beneath, trapped in skeins of wafery
paper-thin skin, lie scintillas of iridescent
sunlight palping the bulb with its poison:

this the forfeit – *ai, ai* –
this the tears.

Acanthus Spinosus: Joe's Love

Decades ago I recall glancing up to see Joe
standing in the living-room doorway,
his arms cradling a sheaf of three feet long
acanthus spears, their graduated racemes
in scales of greyey-white and fading violet
shading down the bracts, and flanked
by two deep green fronds he'd later place
to frame his table arrangement.

That was after hearing how in a snatched
remembrance of his Portuguese boyhood
he'd scaled the abandoned garden wall
to trawl across the lawn and cull armfuls
of this plant as staggeringly handsome as him,
all the time avoiding the needle-fine spines
at the ends of every bloom,
   For don't you know with beauty
   always the pain it comes.

Way back then, we hadn't heard
the myth of Apollo and Acantha –
the forced advance, the rebuff, the torn skin,
and the prick that came between them.
So we had no way of sharing until deaths later,
the truths he'd known all along
of beauty, and its pain. The joys of loving.
Its loss; its gain.

Pear Blossom

Swollen buds at stem-tip
with skin-thin husks,
baby-nail-shaped,

and hints of mint-green leaf,
furred beneath, tacky from sap
that lacquers your hands.

Urgent their burgeoning
in translucent whites, milk-bright,
but tinged with pink stigmata

their faces leaning towards light,
mouths agape in five-petalled keenings:
so many,   so sudden.

And their scent, hanging
over gardens: a headiness
invisibly-heavy

in a pall that summons fruitflies
and bees to knead stamen
and anthers, easing out pollen

with their Spring abandon.
Then a hush of release,
like a gasping after desire

and a wedding-confetti petal-fall
across orchard lawns
in premonitions of Autumn.

The Darkborn

We are a movement, unheard, unseen;
a conspiracy working underground
against the established order of things.

We work secretly, quietly nudging in the dark
to free ourselves, underlings trapped by this earthy state.

This, our aim, we pursue in quiet action:
pushing, taking root, unfelt, unknown to most,
but all the time confusing every plan to keep us down
by brutal feet and force of arm.

And we succeed:
suddenly, in first Spring,
when, quietly and with riotous flowering,
we coltsfoot, common and darkborn,
inherit urgently the sun.

Japanese Anemones

White. And again white.
Like unfired china-ware:
a dusted-down look
of crepe-paper frailness.

Expressionless,
so have you guessing
their territorial ambition
from the tendrils they dare
pushing up clusters of leaf, of stem,
thrusting trios of cushion-buds
unfolding to diadem of petal,
bland inheritors of sun,

and at centre
that satin-covered button
with corona of lemon sepals
stitching everything together.
decades newborn.

So. Are here this year.
Again. Their freshness
already decades ancient.

Rhizome Iris

The border's conquistador

      battling for foothold behind
      lancing palisade of leaf
      and hoisting green spearbud-blades
      through creaming blue to azure
      till maturing to the unfurling purple
      of its full-faced regalia.

The vanquisher of averageness

      its bloom's plush velvet
      pulled from collocations of petal
      and resembling the helmet
      of some sixteenth century halberdier
      in a Titian *Crucifixion* -

      or a slashing axe-head held aloft
      and stunning Summer gardens
      into surrenderings of aahs.

White Phlox

Not Persil-white, but
the kind of white that at petal edge
slides to violet or pastel-lavender
as though holding its own shadow
in their five-petalled fulness of face.

Like bridesmaids gathering in huddles
under full sunlight
it's their quietness that hurts:
that, and the stately catch-glance of their gaze
or when they bow – oh so slightly -
as if admitting an only moment of inclusion
and giving you permission to look.

Otherwise, it's that cold-shouldering
of specialness gone to their heads,
that cool distancing
borrowed from whiteness
and that sticky sweet-sickness smell
that cannot stop them
from giving their presence away.

Kniphofia uvaraia

Nigh-on unpronounceable its botanical label –
too many consonants meted out between
the tripping syllables, and horridly foreign
at that, this immigrant from warmer climes,
deep south in South Africa's western veldt,
that though settled in this Cheshire garden-park
is so amazingly out-of-place it commands attention.

See it ringed with its unforgiving strappy leaves
tapering to nothings as if the sap has clamped
itself down to anchor it, weather-metalled, in earth,
its roots tuberous with anaemic sheen,
a better-than-plastic replica of selfness.

And its flowers, a thrusting up-pushing:
earth's phallus luxuriating in ladderings
of tubular blooms festooning the stem in rosettes
of trumpeting lemon shading through grades
of yellow, amber, orange to resolutions of red –
all a smouldering angriness, the anger of fired iron
that's been withdrawn, and hurriedly, from embers –
so red, so angry with its purposeful
bursting into life that it has left its foreignness
behind, become drawn into our familiar circle
through the measure of our acceptance
and our gift of its common name –
the red hot poker.

Monkshood

Innocent protestors
insisting on standing apart,
outriders in the late Spring border,
already almost a foot above bulbs,
their deep sea-green foliage
a soft, ferny backcloth to other wealths.

See how they hoist their stems
in an indifference to the need for support:
a sturdiness akin to going without
as they perfect strong silhouettes of selfness
against the hedgerow.

And their flowers: true Summer abundance
in an extended length of flowering:
cowls of dense spikes aspiring to skylines
in dusky blues darkening through indigo to navy
and possessing elements of mystery and elegance
almost in redress to their every-bit-toxicity,
as if whispering

We're above all this

Keep
            Right
                    Away

September Sunflowers

Not our six-foot inula
with its intricate whorls of petal-head,
elephant-ear leaves, and serpent stems
we mistakenly named as "English sunflower"

but the real McCoy we logged – is it
twenty years ago now? – in field after
field as driving south through France:
gold, open-faced, and shoulder-height -
you know, those we jokingly doffed
van Gogh's Wunderkind as, living up
to their naming, *tournesol*, they followed
the sun, their heads resplendent, their
yellows heavy in bright sunlight.

Well, yes – these, but not these.
They're Autumnal now. Clown-sad sentinels
fading daily through amber to ochre, then brown,
their leaves drying to brittle flap, and heads
hanging in a sort of sadness
like shrunken old men exchanging
smalltalk on street corners, and eking
out their waiting time.

Garden fern

To start with, looks stonelike:
a thrust of sea-smooth pebbles fisting through;
and then bunched up pinkish knuckles
that bruise the light with their ever-so-slight uncurling –
a temporary aggression in its repertoire of stealth.

Days later, its stems are scaled in bronze
fading away to ginger-russet bristles
which, finger-riffled, feel as plush as pelt, as soft.
And when with Springish certainties,
it hoists up its frond furls,
their heads rising, necks stretching,
like prows of Viking longboats
till suddenly fanning out
with their demanding look-at-me-ness
to hands of pea-green lace –
spaced, fretted, denticulated –
as big as antimacassars
dubbing them "filigree" would be going
over the top; and yet they possess a delicacy
that belies wiry roots worming through layers of earth-dirt.

Could this be how this unputdownable
broadcaster of nowness
unfurling its unexpected declaration of being,
its calculated actuality – urgently, ungently –
survives in the right place /the wrong place.
And why – open-mouthed – the garden

shrinks back into itself
amazed.

Of white foxgloves

Silent leanings,
mouths agape
in a top heavy headiness
like a file of watchers in the hedgerow,
their white, the white of intimate skin.

How the bee fumbles -
his slow probing progress,
his heavy thighs kneading deep
the freckled throat
to her anthers.

And his deflowering withdrawal
spotted and pollen-heavy,
a clumsy lumbering
as if drunk on Summer
and off his head.

Till zig-zags

      to another.

            And another.

Sisters of innocence
their leaning need
like young girls,
fumbled.

How they pout.

James Bateman (1811-97) has his Belief in the Eternal Confirmed by Orchids

Devoted to collecting from aged eight,
Bateman spent a fortune, not to mention
others' lives, satisfying his desires.
So invested days page-grazing
plant catalogues, or rolling the globe
locating places - Guatemala, Surinam –
to trace the plants inhabiting his passion,
till he became entranced by petals
as skin-thin as newborn flesh with its mesh
of skyblue veins barely formed.

How he desired those sublimely white,
their buds like rows of graded baby toes,
their clown-sad eyes lighting brightly
under full sunshine or ghosting through
slow twilights where he lingered, fingering
stems, and smelling their must.

     And how he lusted
after the shockingly exotic in jamborees
of colour from the Creator's palette, almost
frantic in their patterning, so obviously foreign
in enviable beyondness they warmed
his table-talk with the wonders of the Lord.

He could sense their tendrils spreading,
as he strolled past, and their roots - spotty,
blotched – lifting, spidering out, seeking
leverage in the mossy compost, the cradling bark.

And, believing their leaves to be the panting
tongues from the angels of his imagining,
was convinced he could hear their breathing,
so knew, just knew, their petal-wings angled
after him, mouths agape in silent adoration.
His. Theirs. God's making. God's sport.

"Ferns and other flowerless plants came early in the Divine programme, because the coal, into which they were ultimately to be converted had need to be long accumulating for the future comfort and civilization of our race; while the genesis of Orchids was postponed until the time drew near when Man, who was to be soothed by the gentle influence of their beauty, was about to appear on the scene."

James Bateman, Introduction to **Monograph of Odontoglossum**, (1864-74)

Darwin's Orchid: *Angraecum sesquipedela praedicta*

"I have just received such a Box full from Mr Bateman with the astounding *Angraecum sesquipedela* with a nectary a foot long – Good Heavens what insect can suck it."
Charles Darwin to Joseph Hooker, 25th January 1862, **Darwin Correspondence Project**, Letter 3411

Not one of those showily-bold magentas, cerises, oranges,
or those blotched and splodged tri-colours,
just five pea-green buds spanning waxily to green-lined white;
its bi-lobed leaves a deeper green, but leathery;
its trailing roots grey-green, and inflexibly rubbery:
nothing much to write home about. So much green.

But that whip-like spur from where its heady scent –
mixture of cinnamon and honey - spilled into his study
each dusk! Just think, "one-and-a-half-foot"!
It would beggar belief if he hadn't seen it.
And seeing it, worth checking with Hooker
Good Heavens what insect can suck it.
But guessed this nectary was set for cross-pollination.

So, eyeballing at desk-bench level and hand held trembling
tried, and again tried. First, with longish needle.
Next, with thinnest of badger-hair brushes
dipping to springe its pollinia gingerly out.
But fell short, time after time.

Then, inspiration.
Inserted tiniest of cylinders the spur's length,
and retracting – gently, gently, breath held –
found the viscidium attached: pollination possible after all.
But never an insect with such long proboscis!

Until 1903, and Darwin some twenty years dead,
when the Madagascan hawk moth was recorded,
its amber-brown-black wings quivering mid-air,
and backing one foot away, unrolled its proboscis,
then advancing, spritted it into the rostellum-cleft
while gripping the labellum in a six-second drinking.
Once done, lifted head, removed proboscis,
and revealed the attached pollinia.

That was finally that:
Darwin's conviction repaid,
as out of perhapses comes the theory,
comes the poem.

Teasels

Unputdownable
like North country vowels
so have been outlawed to corners
of fields, lay-bys and wasted-space.

See where leaves meet
in basal whorls that shoot upwards
tined with spiny bract and spur of spike
along their strap-like angled stems.

Snap one cracking open
to reveal its milk-white sap,
its insides of fine down
glistening silvery under sun.

Next, measure their Summer treasure
in confections of spherical inflorescence
parading jade to lavender-magenta:
aah, such delicate deception.

Come September, splendour
has gone to their heads:
Celtic-helmeted remnants,
almost barbarian in amber
and bronze, with phalanxes
of hooked tangs and brittle spikes
that match scratches with blood.
Theirs. Yours.
Hacked. Slashed. Cut down.
They're unstoppable.

Next Spring, watch their clans
lancing back over new ground.

Cornflower

there:
a rising nearness, a beacon
its blueness a raggy topknot mix
of indigo, azure and violet
that humbles you to silence
as you stumble across its sudden fulness
signalling from wheat-field trespass

Consider its other names:

> *Hurtsickle* from its tough stems -
> that angelicaed haze of greyey-green
> blunting the reaper's scythe

> *Cyanus*, memento of the garland
> his namesake garnered as a lad
> to frame his love for Flora

> *Centaurea*, after Chiron the centaur
> who swathed Hercules' poisoned arrow-wounds
> in braids of sky-blue petal-heads
> and was healed

Remember these
and recall this flower
the single bloom to grow in Nagasaki's aftermath
                             Hiroshima's wreath

Cornflower,
talisman of hurt, of youth, of hope

Fireside Survivors

Ovoid like Zulu warrior shields,
but gleaming with the sheen of glycerine
and distinctive in that mix of ginger,
mahogany and Titian red,
they straddle cultures, span civilizations,
know only resurgence.

Remember Mum telling the legend
of spending her honeymoon week,
night after night, by the fireside
in their Rupert Street home, and Dad
bashing and crushing with flat-iron
as she poured scalding water
on these brittle scabs – *Little buggers
must have numbered hundreds –*
only to do the same. Again. Again …

And my wife's Dad larding the saga
of earning pin-money from his landlord
by filling with mortar the gaps
between floor and wall and skirting-board –
Thought they'd come through Lil's party-wall –
till saw them scrabbling from fire-ash
beneath his black-leaded range,
their shielded backs reddy-amber
like the embers they trod …

Then recall that the single species
          antennae testing temperature,
          feet trekking charred territory
to survive Nagasaki's furnace intact
was *Periplaneta Americana,*
the household cockroach.

Happening on Dragonfly

See the rhythm of its being:
a performance that claims attention
momentarily.

Its flight the jewellery of music
how it balances on air.
Lingers. Settles to rest

till possessed by the andante
of its being, then shivers away,
this quicksilver confection

of turquoise and amethyst,
this near brooch
that denies possession.

But, for sure, no one can own it
with its nearly-there-ness
of thin-as-June-mist wings.

Then again, you wouldn't think
anyone would want its chainmail fuselage,
its pug-ugly face,

the bulging eyes as if blinded
by its own Japanese-lacquered glare,
its sea-green sheen,

yet how the heron stills it bill,
its greyness a discordant undertone
in this insect's colour symphony ...

Scarlet Lily Beetle (*Lilioceris lilii*)

Almost jackal-faced, this Anubis
of the garden border, with its
black-capped antennae, its notched
black eyes topping the hard-backed

forewings, the scarlet of Japanese
lacquer-ware. Somehow alien,
it overwinters in darkness, under
ground. And, in early Spring,

feelers its way through humus
and leaf-litter to emerge, antennae
radaring in on lily and fritillary,
their sappy leaves, buds and stems.

Lays swathes of eggs on beneaths
of leaves, kept safe from predators
by a fuzz of sticky brown frass
as its larvae fatten before burrowing

underground to pupate in darkness.
Climbing back to light again,
is adept at hiding inside leaf-cleft
and whorl of bud. Threatened,

is reckoned by experts to squeak
against predation, rubbing its parts
in stridulation. So, approaching it,
it goes into the pose of thanatos;

withdrawing its six stilted legs;
and falling in a sort of forward
roll down ladders of leaf bract
to land with its black undersurface

facing upwards, helping it melt
into indistinction against soil.
Almost unputdownable, malathion
cannot rumble its multiplication;

only postpone. Your best bet in
defence is handpicking, and crushing
between fingers, or crunching underfoot
with your eyes shut. Listen to the crack

of its back, its elytra shattered
like eggshell, its inners spilled,
and its redness spread to pity.

Consider, then, this is God's gift, too.

History's Footnote: the fly

For much of the time goes unnoticed
even when, after his zigzag tantivying,
he draws near and lands four-squarely
almost in your face, to stand silently,
legs angled and straddled like a riderless
horse, but littler than miniature.

So no wonder folk dismiss him
as insignificant, this irritant marauder
clad in his oil-skin blackness with glintings
picked out in slices of light from the dullest
shudders of under-colours verging on
Prussian blue and indigo.

Watch him rinsing his hands
this Uriah Heep of the dunghill,
then sleeking them down his old man cheeks,
grooming his moustache, slicking whiskers,
and brushing back the sides of his head
as if mussing his hair,
all the time holding the rest of himself still,
his bobbled eyes not letting on
his history owns catalogues
of blood, of open wounds, of sores.

He doesn't even begin to list
the piles of detritus he's visited.
Or acknowledge that his CV
registers it was his milling siblings

that hosted the ceremonies
when Cromwell was resurrected
and his severed head hoisted
above pikestaff at Tyburn Hill
and the air was bizzingly-filled
with wars and rumours of wars …

Hive

This is the whited sepulchre.

At its portals, honeybees,
head hung in supplication,
inch through half-darkness
towards the inner sanctum.

Assembled throngs
drone their undersong.

Attended by unsexed priestesses,
the old matriarch, She-to-die-for,
presides in the half-light.

She waxes fat
on their golden oblations
fresh from their covenant
with the sun.

She adores their adorings.
The air is a-buzz with praise.

In the darkness
of their hexagonal cells
her acolytes are multiplying.

Her service, their need.

The Queen Bee Speaks

Am too worn now for swarming,
so have made death untenable
with devotions to giving birth.
My being is egg-machine.

Every minute brings addition:
white sliding capsules
each cocooned to a honeycomb
in the round skep's assembly-gloom.

My handmaidens - uncountable
hundreds – are bent on virginity,
their genitalia traded for tail-end regalia
crowned with stings of hooks.

Spinsters insistent on innocence,
they suckle the nursery larvae
on royal jelly, go questing for nectar
in replication of selves.

Are secretive: hold the whereabouts
of clover, of heather hidden in the riddles
of their zizzing dance.

Deep indoors, conspiracies
of drones interrogate their sex
in election of fathering
the next queen.

The sole use of males
is divining patrimony.
Feeding their machinations on may-bes,
I keep them on hold.

Uncle A Takes Up Beekeeping

his get-up ridiculously over-the-top,
precaution against those stings he's seen atolling limbs
in photographs, but then no bigger than sixpenny bits
with pink rings like a kid-goat's nipples:

so has bought these gauntlets, in white,
the sort worn by stevedores – thick, padded –
that trick fingers all to thumbs;
a wide-brimmed hat – again in white – with trailing
veil that shows up grey against the light;
and massy overalls, also in white, slickly zipping
up the front, buttoning at cuffs, and tucking into
dullwhite gumboots that have him galumphing as he walks.

(Says he needed white so's not to frighten the bees –
  would make him statuesque as a tree, difficult to see.)

He looks some surgeon – distant, removed –
as if he should be operating behind glass,
busy with some bigger thing, not these delicate specimens,
brooch-little in their precious ambers and golds,
easy to unpin, or crush, casually, underfoot …

Looks a giant - huge, and other-worldly -
set against this heaving hive at knee-height, fizzing busily
like fusing wire in an angry bizzing as if the box
is about to explode any moment, the wood so vulnerable,

and him unsuspecting how this ancient order
where one Queen reigns supreme, unseen,
has minds on other things –
a swarming that will make him run for cover,
enslave him to her whims ...

Points of Reference

My wife finds comforting the cicadas' mating-calls.
I choose the river's quieter sibilants, as it pieces itself together,
syllable by syllable, voicing its being
out loud like a child reading: *I talk therefore I am.*

Those practised aspirants angling through dragging
hands, those hard consonants gravelling gutturally
round its tongue, pushing its plosive pluck and pulls,
flattening, then opening its vowels till it finds
its glottal stops, slapping its wet voice against me,
calling me to walk with its day-whine, its sun-song.

Its syntax pulls others: damsel and dragonflies,
rainbowed trout, kingfisher, roach. They too have
their sentences in its autobiography.
Do I have a part? Or am I incidental
like its name on my map, in blue,
squiggly-insignificant and indexed for easy-reference?

Sometimes I envy my wife's greater sense:
her truths kept open like the cicadas' tzinging in the trees,
her thoughts, like them, buttoning up as you draw close,
sharing themselves between themselves and darkness.

Red Admirals

Pulsing heart-beats,
the isms of being; almost iambic
their blood-tick, their wing-tick –
break flash / break flash

or outstaring the day-gaze
with a vermilion blaze
upon black: the colours of poppy.

Long-tongued, seeking
the speed of flowers –
getting high on it, higher, higher,
a drugged, stumble-flight
up at the moor's edge
with its milk-thistles, its knapweed.

(Is it purple that pulls them?)

Or gardened with trailing
skeins of buddleia (their scattered
flashes like girls parading
headfuls of hair-slides)
sudden savagery in our town;
a native face-mask, stabbing
from greenness – a pirate-slash,
a stirring of groin.

Are the splayers of flowers,
caressing petals, and stamens,
feasting their isness, their futures
with the kneading-keenness of sex.

Closed-up, are paper wafers
of bark, or Cape Triangles
of good hope. (Many the nets
we kids broke; and jam-jars
a day-or-two jungle with
blades of grass and strangled
flowers. Even then, amidst cup-handed
flutter, that out-facing, out-daring
blazon of colour gave us
tastes of excitement – the sudden
blood-bursts of cuts, that pain
of amazement.

Ageing, we add
fragilities of life,
the nothingnesses of life.)

Red Admirals, captains
of ships of youth, harbingers
of sad passages, of death.

God's other toys.

A timeless heraldry

The butterflies are free … Charles Dickens, ***Bleak House***

Released from marooning cocoons
where they've lain cramped
in that paper-dry, leaf-like chrysalis,
see how, with their old man shoulder-shrugs,
their questing heads have tested
the fresh Spring air – legs unhinging
like deckchairs unwrapped from winterings,
and gently flexing their curled tapestries
of wings, are edging to confidence
in a sort of under-colour
like the hardly-there pattern of turned back rugs:
a subduedness – till begin unreeling their antennae
to clean down their shrimpfish faces,
crimped and lean.

Look how they shake their wings
gingerly against light – again gingerly,
in a hesitant tremble like sieving flour,
till unburdening the dull months of crumple –
and flish! – they inherit patternings
planted aeons ago, blazoning now, here, today –
the scarlet, amber, black and white
of Red Admirals – flashing a timeless heraldry
that knows only allegiance to self,
announcing *I am here. See me. See me. I am free* …

Unaware that within days
their me-ness will be spent;
their freedom gone.

Garden startled

as dredging through September vegetation –
trimming heuchera leaves (their bruised maroons
lipped in vermilion) – I'm surprised by craneflies
suddenly rising – One… Two… Five – edging
over leaf's edge and staggering in a sort of drunken
lurch, apprising their horizons to go helicoptering,
out, and up – sashaying, legs trailing in a cradling flight,
their lean fuselage draping behind, and silently climbing,
till levelling out, circling, down, round and
dipping, one by one to settle on the lawn –
their old men's faces greyly straight-laced
like imams intent on prayer ….

And I'm reminded of that film-clip
with jungle under morning mists, trees
top-brushed by sun – a heaven-lit rose-blush benediction –
and skimming helicopters rising out of high palms,
a swooping arcing lift, rocking and swaying,
then swinging in to circle the river's broad sweep,
s-bending, silver in the sun, and pushing on, over,
camera-panning tracking them,
making them bigger, big in their storming formation
as banking and dipping - with all the time,
their hacking sound drowned out by film's soundtrack –
Wagner's *Ride of the Valkyries*
in Coppola's *Apocalypse Now* …

And am startled again
by contiguities of imagination
with matters of fact.

Of craneflies

Fidgety scribblers,
their Jack Frosty wings
all a-twitch, in a flickering
so quick as if they're nibbling
at daylight, trying to rub it out,
and darkness is what they're after,
night-time all they need.

Stick-fine their body
and rough-raw as tedded straw,
their hinged back legs trailing
like a heron's after lift-off.

Pairs of them, tail ends
locking on in something close
to a strangler's manhold,
as feeding their need.
Jigging at it
as if they can't get enough.

Then shifting to drift apart.
And up. Away.
Rising, climbing, legs dangling
in a mad-angled dance,
till tumbling
to a falling stall,
stage by step, by stage

and dibbing at ground
with that bobbing jolt
as at the hangman's behest.

Death so sudden. So near.

Revisiting Sheelagh's Way With Baked Trout

Remember liberty-bodice buttons?
Those brittle yellow-become-ochre discs,
ungiving and pebble-like. So this eye.
Empty. Done to death. No feeling in it.
Enough to make you guilty. Just a staring
blankness that matches the dulled flank
of its being, so different from when living
with its silvery-gleam, its shimmering is-ness,
its metallic self.
            Instead, this baked, flaky
range of scales. Its spoilt-child pouting mouth.
Gills, fin, tail – all held as if in use, but kept
separately. Stilled. Almost twigish.

So it was when first you showed us how
to peel back the flesh from the ladder
of bone, taking clear away its white spines
from the rake of vertebrae to free the skeins
of its pink innernesses where congealed smudges
of blood had underwritten its living.

That's why today we're not fazed
by this ceremonial dish of baked fish.
Know how to tackle this package of skin,
of bone, of flesh. Our single regret
is that you're no longer here to share it.
Your eyes hard; your limbs twig-like.
All done to death.
            Just guilt pricking
the back of the throat, like a missed
fishbone we cannot shift that's bringing
tears to our avoiding eyes.

Bodyboarders, Newgale Beach

for Adam, Toby & Katy

Straddling the almost nothingness
of surfboard and kitted out in wetsuits,
they're self-silhouettes, liquorice-flicked.

Beneath them lies temptation,
its sea-swell lulling them to buoyancies:
the rise, the fall, the drift.

Waves are their bounty
as riding the incoming tide,
their faces recording their nowness –

the dare, the fun, the fear.
How profligately
they caress its crests,

their fingers raking the spume,
sifting its chilled veins, its sand,
its shell-shingle

to riddled stillnesses.
See how the beach greets them
where they towel their wetness down.

Try as they might,
they cannot wipe away
that salt-birth slick on their lips.

Lads Diving at Stainforth Force

Its plunge a froth-ringed stout,
this waterfall is alluring;
and these youths so drunk on it,
they cannot leave it alone, but dive,
and out, and dive, again, again,
light-headed in addiction's frenzy.

Sharp-cut like playing-cards,
shoulders held square above jaunty swimming shorts,
and torsos thickening to manhood,
they launch themselves from the limestone ledge.

Once they've tackled its twelvefoot
dive, they've no real fear, but are magnetised
by the forty, fifty, sixty feet of chilled riverings
they cannot hope to penetrate, let alone own,
deeper even than their imaginings, –
are finding the depths of their courage
in the depths of the river,
each out-daring the rest,
searching minds to discover
their own depths, by downing their limbs
in the river's limbs as they plunge and swim,
and climb and plunge.

Already some are wearing the shadows of my frame –
broad-beamed with too much sitting,
roll-shouldered from too much writing.

Perhaps in years to come,
watching out on banksides,
they'll grow to accept their fears, like men.

Mussels

Abandoned shells stranded on the shore
sporting their washed-out denims,
their bluey-grey hasbeens.

Turn them, their nacreous abalone
is a February morning sky,
the pink sheen of dawn,
the silver-streaked sea.

And, there, nestling - wetted
unopened - in rock pools
a specialness of indigo, sable and navy,
sparking like a starling's shell-bladed wings.

Take them. Make them open:
this hinged bivalve its own Siamese twin,
its membrane like cross-sectioned ovaries
offered for inspection.

Touch that fish-slippery give
of flesh within, its rubbery foot
nipple-pink and fringed with tangerine.

Mussels, the stuff of the Atlantic
carrying the tang of evolution.
Their being, our fill. Our greed.

Beached Jellyfish

This near-transparent plodge stranded
at sea's lip is an upturned Lalique platter,
its centre the smoky-blue of water-thinned milk
set in an haloed rim, clearer and as cold
as glass but rubbery, with the littlest of give
as if resisting inroads.

And yet, it's no way collectible,
this reckoning of negation
that possesses no visible inner machinery;
no twitching lymph; no blood; no skin; no face;
nothing that resembles an eye or ear.
And no response when prodded;
though it gives a squish and sluck
when eased with nudging Croc or stick.

Keeping it alive's the tricky thing.
Too massy by half for kid's plastic spade,
it's slippery-difficult in lifting - slides
over the side, collapsing flatly, and
splatting on sand. And mustn't touch
with hand or foot. So best to leave it
islanded there, kept wet by deepings
of beach-bucketed sea.

Then, if it survives till the turn of tide,
this *Medusa* will meld with the pulsing shunt
and push of its trailing veils
into a full-moon face
ghosting through prehistory's galaxy.

But, for the now, herring-gulls are gathering.

Window-ledge with Herring-gull

Background first:
to the right, the sea:
a silver-white slice just under the horizon
then a wedge of metal grey

And, left, the same colours borrowed by the pier:
its silver oriental cupolas, its metalled web –
stilts, trusses, cross-rails –
in grey to black: a starkness

Foreground now:
a beauty of a gull, its pure white and grey
so perfectly balanced,
the grey smudging like cirrus cloud:
sort of feathery - which is what it is -
and pink flat feet, the pink of pink plastic,
and mapped out in a triad web
with an after-thought of a hind-spur kicking in

How keen its bead-eye; and nervy its head
in that tick, and tick – this way, that –
not rolling like the slowness of the ocean's tides,
or even the leverage of its spearing beak

And, suddenly, I'm aware that the horizon –
that pencil line out at sea, dividing sea's
khaki-greyey-green from grey of sky –
that the horizon is not a straight line,
but curved: a slow downturned arc, barely there

No wonder the flat-earthers believed the world
just another ledge to drop off
rather than a window
to understanding other things

Not even a sparrow

We've seen them at a distance
this motley flock
like a handful of crumbs
thrown into the wind:
up, swirl, drift, rush, down
and gone

But this is different,
this singleton at close up,
so still, unmoving
after his chimney-flue fall

his lustre-ware feathers
a speckled treasury, soot-dusted

his twig-thin claws
like fine cracks in china

the hook of his nails

his gawping beak
soundless now

And over the furniture
a galaxy of splatter
where he zagged
his freedom flight
in his panic dance of death
the length and torment
of our living-room

Twitching Sixers: *A First Clutch*

I   Magpie strutting his stuff. This way. That.
         Braggart of the managed hayfield.
         Till - flash - unravels the black and white
         banner of himself
         chak-chaking our sorrow
         flagging our joy.

II   Mallards battling in a gaggle
         overhead, madly whanging
         till a sudden baulk, and tip,
         wing dangling at right angle
         like an anchor
         dropping fast to land.

III   Starling at fledgling level
         just another grey-brown thing of a bird.
         Couple of months on becomes
         masquerading popinjay in his layered regalia:
         nacreous jewel of the shrubbery,
         our garden's pearl.

IV   Woodpigeon flap-scrabbling
         and laddering high, suddenly cutting
         engine to fall to stalled self silhouette
         mindlessly gliding till faffing back
         to letching again, refuelling
         his *Coo-oo-oo want you. Want you-ou.*

V   Crow, clad all in black, swaggerer
         of some backyard Jacobean Tragedy.
         The cadaver's surgeon, how he stoops.
         Strops. Stabs. His cronking tally
         seeding his eye glint, his pinion-winged
         sleekness. Greed, his need.

VI   Goldfinch, nervy-alert at the bird-feeder.
Head pecking, then checking frenetically.
Left. Right. He's that uptight, doesn't know
his body's yo-yoing and the flash
of black, of red, of gold's a give-away –
the twitching gone to his head.

VII   Falcon gliding on thermals
swooping, circling
apparently wingless
is a stringless Chinese kite.
What irony.
A kite like a kite.

VIII   Pheasant, the lane's jay-walker,
tempting treasurer of feather.
Winter's nimble side-stepper
become Summer month's
hit and run victim,
feather-mess of road kill.

IX   Returning blackbird
coming again, again
in the violet twilight
back to the ivy, and feasting its need
on the berries, purple-black,
the sheen of its back feathers, its bill.

Blackbird Paternity

Running under his shoulders,
he skulks between lupins
like a back-alley cat, sneakily
busy with its own business.

He's intent on survival: his,
and a nest full of brats elbowing
scrawnily in their new day down,
their beaks rawly gaping.

Now, once out into the open,
he's posing mid-lawn, as if
he doesn't care he's grounded,
and suddenly vulnerable.

So, flaps wings, trips forward,
seed eyes alert, head alert.
Stops. Bobs. Flacks tail twice.
Trots along. Stops. Stabs.

This is his version of some
Black Crow tribal dance,
his totem the token grub,
struggling, and dangling

in his mud-streaked beak
like mayoral chains:
a ritualistic livery he wears
all his day long.

From the beech hedge,
fledglings yawp for victuals.
Greed their need.
Of such is paternity.

A January morning haunting

Read yesterday how redwings perish
in huge numbers during severe Winters
when ground is too frozen to dig for food.
So wasn't in the least surprized to see
this morning by the front porch this redwing.
Dead. Stiff as the proverbial board, lying
sideways, flank flashed in russets,
chest speckled in splendid regalia –
the ochre/amber feathers, flecks of brown,
the slicing whites. Its beak agawp, and eyes
like stones set in their white eye-stripe,
their light long gone out. And claws curved
inwards. Legs deck-chair hinged.

Thinking nothing much, brushed it aside
with side-swipe of boot, until later,
then shovelled it up and dumped its dead lump
under the roadside hedge.

But was haunted the rest of the week
by thoughts of the way we treat our old folk.
Much the same, bundling away.
But without shovel. Or hedge.
Let alone a poem.

On A Wood Pigeon Proposition

When you catch a glance of it tantivying across
the garden, its wings battling forward/back
like the oars of the Oxbridge boat race as if all
that really mattered is the winning, and you notice
how the new-dawn-pink blush of neck and chest,
the smoky greys of its back, the whitish slash
at back of its neck, have been watered down
against the sun to a charcoaled silhouette ...

                      and when it sails
like a child's paper plane racing over the lawn, then
lifts to a clattering ladder of mad flapping and stalls,
its wings akimbo like those cliff-hurlers launching midair
into vacancies of space in a sort of death-daring
that has your heart in your mouth, and not landing –
but gliding, tight breasted, wide - rising, falling,
then arcing in to wing-drift to the leylandii,
or flop-dropping to settle on the trellis ....

                      and when it stoops
wing-crash-flapping on the garden steps its head
tick-tocking as if on clockwork, its seed eyes mad-panicking,
its bill's rolled gold, those coral pink toes, and communing
in its jewellery-plumage puts on its song
like a stuck recording, *Coo-oo-cou, Love-you ...*

                         then you know
this is me, is you, is us - that lift, that dive, that fall,
the battling mad clatter of our love that has my heart
in my mouth just seeing you ...

Coo-oo-cou ... Love-you ...

Two days after the lashing storm

we woke to the swallows' return. We had missed
their mad-cap skimming over the swimming pool,
the way they dipped, wings almost clipping

the cool water, and, afterwards, their gatherings
on the telegraph wires. Without them, the sky had seemed
menacingly bare, so it was a relief seeing them once more:

black flecks high against the cloud line, flickering
in a dazzling clip and lift, an arcing slice against light,
and, later, zipping once again over the pool's meniscus.

They couldn't be the same birds, surely? Perhaps others,
rendezvousing before their southern sortie ... Either way,
sure sign things were beginning to return to normal.

And there, foraging amongst walnut trees, golden orioles
their yellow indistinct till flight, with flashes of lemon
brightening against blue. And, on the barn wall,

the sunlight dressing the chrome stone and mortar,
bonding them into a self-emblem, charcoaled almost
to its own capturing caricature – another near

perfection that could not be held. It was then I recalled
what you'd said closing the bedroom-door behind you
Possession is not love, remember. It isn't love.

Considering the First Noticed Visit of Bullfinches
to the Garden

He so cocksure, announcing arrival
and broadcasting his manifesto
on his chest – orange-become-pink –
and posing like some mid-eastern sheik
trawling his wares at the souk:
Come, look. How can you ignore me.
See my burnished breast.
My handsome black cap.
My barred wings.
My flight tails.
This is my being.

She, pecking secondary,
as if holding back
three paces behind the mullah.
Her plumage those faded shades
of Levantine carpets – eastern, distant:
the blush fuddling of breast feather,
those grey-pink downs brushed
by touches of olive and crushed mulberry
and rippling under sunlight like shot silk
in an altogether no nonsense reckoning
of this is what it is to be seen to be subservient.
It's sufficient to be.

And me in my dull garb and pale face
caught in my pride in this instance
as mindful I'm merely gardener,
the overseer of Nature. How can I match
such splendour.
        So stand, and gawp.
And hope they'll be back again and again
before the Fall.

Song Thrush

A thrush sings, his yellow-ochre bill
held high and trilling as if pulling
the tune from deep down within him,

and up through blood, veins, arteries
to his speckled breast where it circles
his chirring heart, his chest feathers rising

and falling till fit to burst, and the song
almost liquid as though each note has
been calibrated from the morning dew

and refined by the early sunlight
to burble out, announcing his arrival:
this survivor of April rain and winds.

His head cocking, and with almost a smile
in that bead of an eye, he's chortling,
look at me ... look at me .... look at me, now.

From which primer has he stolen this song?

Who wrote the score for his aria?

Who applauds his encore?

City Pigeons

Nobody-owned slatterns of streets and
public spaces, they're ace at strutting their stuff
in that fat-man waddle, all the time head-pecking
the scattered seeds, and parading their shades
of smutty grey, except when blades of sunlight
catch their neck-feather wealth,
its aquamarines, violets, mauves, emerald greens
ripple-shimmering like spilt petrol pools after rain.

And when they lift, twenty-plus together
as if there's only one brain shared between them,
their wings swishing like crashing surf, and they circle
wheeling round, and back, caught up in the thrown scarf
of themselves, looping and turning, knotting themselves through
and back again, the neat black triangles of their wings
clip-clipping fast, tantivying hell-for-leather as if
this mad panicky show is all they need to know –
then is when the sunlight suddenly tips their underwings
and twitches them in flickerings of white
like glistening crystals of snow.

Nightjar

for John Booth

I   Just watch. And listen

Honeyed Summer-evening,
the soporific light hazy with midges and flies,
sky wide open but with a threat of cloud,
and sun slowly lowering,
the horizon blushing through lemon-yellows
to pink, and rose, before a final full-bloodied
smudge of twilight.

We've parked the car, climbed through
two sheep-fields, over stiles, and found,
behind the hedge, the purlieu of bracken
and gorse keeping farmland apart from wilderness
and demarking the edge of the felled conifer plantation,
with Scots pine, and larch beyond.

Binocs ready, we settle down, tuning in
to the balmy evening bizz of insects, the burblings
of late birds, swish of wing, rattled branch.
We are all ears in this busy myriad world.

And *twisick*. And again *twisick*
rings through the clear evening
igniting our fizz of anticipation.
Woodcock, you say. *Woodcock.*
Just watch. And listen.

Now there's a distant drilling *trr-trr-trr-derrr-er*
as of wood suffering under milling-bit,
or a Geiger-counter identifying
trr-trr-trr-derrr-er – seems like minutes –
trr-trr-trr-derrr-er louder, then fading, rising and
falling, and lifting in a distinctive insistency.

You say, *Nightjars. That's nightjars churring ...*
and through the near-dark come skimming shapes
on long angled wings, twisting and bounding
in buoyant flight – the barred markings of nightjar ...

Too soon, full darkness falls
and, hooded by night's star-spangled cowl,
we gingerly pick our way back to the car,
spirits uplifted, our heads ringing with

trr-trr-trr-derrr-er   trr-trr-trr-derrr-er

And your words ...
Just watch. And listen.

II   Goatsucker

His delicate featherings
with the marvels of barred plumage
make bark his ally, this sallier
of morning's dawn
and near dark.

See him silently twilighting –
his twists, his turns –
his pointed wings and kestrel-shaped tail
as hawking for food,
this moth- and beetle-eating machine,
flying, beak open-wide
as if to compensate
for his snub-nosed bill
with its bristled fringe.

Hear his churring,
rising and falling,
disturbing the still Summer dusk.
Hear his insistent coo-ic coo-ic call.
The whip-crack of his flapping wing.

But in the daytime
you might overlook his silent hiding
among bracken and gorse,
his own still-life
placed in the earth-scrape nest,
and passing off self
as leaf-litter and bark-shard

his stillness and secrets,
his goat-sucking
long gone to ground
with Pan.

Starlings, gathering

Late September afternoon – five-thirtyish.
Light, thin – almost fragile.
Sky, clear, and clean as a china plate.
Sunshine, hazy, but still warm on your back.

And there, two – no, three – starlings. Not
close at hand on the back-garden steps so you
can see the chainmail of their breast feathers
shining like flecked Japanese lacquering
in their amethysts, violets, jades, golds;
not see their almost head-checking insolence,
their dead-eye stare, dismissive;
not see their citrine beaks, their lemon legs –
no, not near enough to catch such detail
but jetting through sky like kids' paper darts,
their silhouettes trimmed clear, sharp, dark
as they tantivy out of sight, circle once, and
back, wings battling, then coast in a long,
slow glide, till picking up wings again
in a frantic flapping, and soar, circling round,
the trio of them as if on a mission.

And suddenly, sharply, two, three, four more.
No. Five. Six – striking in from all angles:
black arrowheads, streamlined to efficiency,
joining in and carving through air their balletic
curve – soaring, rising, wheeling, swooping –
as if showing off to each other, jockeying
for position, the lead shifting one to another,
then another, passing the baton in a game
somehow casual, but underwritten by need.

And there, a further wave, upwards of thirty
careering in from the East. Holding line, riding
high. In unison, again. And round. Round
in encircling scoops, weaving, wrapping
the loop of themselves around themselves,
and gathering the rest, hurtling together
towards murmuration, as the light slides away,
the sun turning orange-red, the far horizon burning.

Where do all the birds go

when they die. Not eventually that is,
but at the exact check of death. Like now. Just now.
Expect you've recognised that dead
they're rarely seen. Nothing left on lawns even:
no beak, no claws, no feather-down, no bone.

Yes, I know there are other places, other times
        (think roadkill - pheasants mainly -
        zigzag-hassled and shattered in smudges
        of plumage and runs of blood;
        there's the odd brown job, too –
        sparrow, dunnock, wren –
        cat-trophied home and left on doorsteps;
        and crows hanging black-binliner-bags
        in rows on the barbed-wire fence)
but where, I ask you, do the rest go ...

No lying in state for the King of birds - the convocation.
No session recess for the parliament of owls.
No sentence for the clamour of rooks,
the unkindness of ravens, deceit of lapwings,
scold of jays.

Nothing seen of the glaring of owls, their wisdom,
the congregation of plovers,
the wake of buzzards,
the piteousness of doves.
Not to mention the exaltation of larks
as high as kites;
and as for the lamentation of swans - so heavy, so big -
no sign at all.

So where do the birds ... Where do they go ...

Like distant cousins in foreign parts, or spinster great aunts
who is at their committal, their internment ...
Where is there any remembering ...

Where do they all go ...

Perfecting your collection

Experts reckon it's just a matter of the application
of scientific principles – you know,
a question of material resistance,
theorems of leverage, force field and penetration,
a concatenation of surface angle, tensions, motion, speed,
et cetera, et cetera

Nothing at all to do with how you stretch
your hands through hedgerows, questing between
stems, between twigs, angling around bud, leaf,
letting fingers imitate the insights of eyes
till settling on ceremonies of egg,
this precious treasure, this testament to existence

then, making sure you're not taking
the lot, pincering and gingerly lifting one,
up, over the nest's rim, and down, still warm
where, holding it chest-level between thumb
and index finger, picking a barb
      hawthorn spurs, their brown-madders
      tipped in crimson, are best
and, pricking with pinholes
the shell at each end, bringing it to lips,
blowing in an almost mimicry of kissing
slow   gentle   strong   long
till albumen, then finally yolk
skein away in liquid glistenings

and you're left with this trophy of hollowness,
an emptiness that's one step nearer
to perfecting your collection,
this making a kill

Foxed

Though it's coal-dark on the moor
with only your walking-lamp to guide you
you see him – well, nearly – the redness
of his pelt melting to indistinction.

It's the brightness of his eyes caught
by lamplight that you first sight: the way
they move – hurriedly, then still, till he
runs again, trottingly.
                              Stops. A moment.
Off again, a skittering. Stops. And still.

And then a sudden flurry as sliding silently
by the stone wall, trying to become the wall,
using its line and curve as cover, as torn
between being trapped between wall and road,
so slinking as if insignificant, as if not there,
yet alive to any chance of staying alive.

So, picks up running again, sheepishly
in a one-two-step, then stop, and spring
scrambling jack-flapping over stone, up
over the wall – and gone, in a flash, and
as suddenly, the darkness collapses
back into ordinariness

Gift-horse

Imagined it hunkering there,
innocently inquisitive to begin with,
its jaw rolling horizontally, its nose twitching
in its foraging, the sunshine gracing its pelt
and dressing it yellow with hazy drizzles of light
that shimmied the length and back again of its flanks
like the rippling muscles of some sumo wrestler.

I sensed, though, it wouldn't stay in full view
but would vanish itself away
into that orange-brown smudge of a thing
sliding by the green-tipped hawthorns
and through the barbed-wire spikes,
till slipping back out into the open,
its white clump of scut
flashing against dark tarmac.

It couldn't have known then – could it? –
how it would be magicked into a dull lump
like a pile of bricks, its limbs twisted
in a child's plasticine caricature of itself;

its soft hair, the silk-softness
of its flap-ears and underbelly
gradually growing as wiry
and lifeless as candyfloss;

and from its head, that dribbled spill of red
shading away to purple
and hardening blue-black under the sun.

You wouldn't think this unwrapped package
much of a gift, though I'd thought it yours
right from the moment I imagined its presence
as piecing the words together
in this my written-off road-kill …

So, take it. Take it now.
It's yours for keeps …

The Last Irish Elk

cornered by steel-eyed cold and drilling wind,
found his bulk a handicap against such skilled opponents.

Sinking their teeth into him, they left him nothing to charge,
nothing to launch reeling backwards,
then upwards into the air.

The more he threshed and scythed,
the more they cut him down to size.
Antlers became ornament, so much useless tree
to drag around that at times he almost became rooted.
They would have had him on his knees,
but with eyes steeled to the future
he could only think of running.

Body was a drum where terror
played irregular fugues
with his bloodbeat. Ribs conspired,
clubbing him from inside.
Panic grew a dynamo that drove him
plunging, back-tracking,
side-stepping, a sort of tragic last-tango.
Eyes rolling widely, he tried all directions.
Legs splayed, pulling him first this way, then that,
would have gone four ways at once
had they been free agents
but were tied so tightly to his body
they were hamstrung.
Heart burned, and knocked.
Saliva spilled and frothed.
It was sheer panic. And sweat.

Till from body's four corners,
places unknown till now,
came a groan, tearing through stretched neck,
spilling over curved lips, between each yellow tooth,
a groan born from his forefathers' pietas,
summary of all Elk's misery since Creation.

It was then, that lunging a final escape,
he burst his lungs, snagged a fragile shank on a careless rock
and blood and dribbled spit from his lips,
blood from his leg, zigzagged his despair,
patterning the ground where his life ran out,
starring a fresh galaxy on the land,
mapping the last of his line.

Fighting he became stone
became stone

and ice took up cartography.

Moles are holy

I   Are soil's impassioned disciples
pursuing their mission with blind faith
as they push everything to their conversion.

Suited to the task in clerical black
they begin as underground movement
and gradually bring their message with them.

You can measure their gospels' success
by the ground they have gained.

II   And after mole-trappings
when they're swinging on barbed-wire
their temples become so many Golgothas.

You wonder why they keep continuing.
Surely by now you'd think they'd have learned
prophets are never recognised in their own land
and evangelism nearly always spurned.

III   When Paul Homes Development
called in JCBs to heap up the ground,
moles abandoned the unequal competition:
not even mole-God could match steel-claw's challenge.

Six years on, gardens flattened,
soil controlled, wilderness tamed,
our neighbours fear moles might return
to stake out their homes with rebellious earth.

We alone would feel honoured
that the moor has begun our acceptance
in its new birth.

Defining Boundaries

Not drystone walling with its stone bones
netting hillsides and moorlands
as shepherding the pasture-land
with its meadow foxtail, its field timothy grass
under the loneliness of exposed skies
and the curlew's liquid drill.

Not this, but that arrangement
of attendant boundary-trees
strappy alders with their leaf-shoals,
flat-handed sycamores, beeches, oaks,
the briar, bramble, and wild dogrose
and, most of all, the hawthorn
with its aniseed pall, its blood berries,
its rise and fall, twists and dips
mirroring the land's arteries.

So there's no gainsaying
what's to be gained by the layering of limbs –
hacking, nicking, chopping, splicing
slice by slice –
till taking the naked stems
and twining them,
the sap-ichor weeping
from their wound-raw cuts.

No, not ungiving stone.
But the trees about you and the layerings of hawthorn
whose give-and-take of limbs
conspire to define our boundaries,
and celebrate our tryst.

Re-Building the Drystone Wall

To begin with, what's already there
needs knocking down. Yes. Take that
distressed thing apart, stone by stone
and if you think it'll help to make
things easier, stack the boulders by shape
and size - watch your toes, though.

But whatever else, to pull off a real
good job you need to do your level best
to make the ground-base flat. So start
from scratch, and clear out the earth-dirt.
And the rubble. (A handbrush and spade,
or pointed masonry-trowel might help.)

Now the building. The problem's always
where to begin. Don't be feart. Take heart.
Pick a block of stone – heavy, solid, squat -
(the more sizeable the better) and manhandle
it into place. Then to stop things budging
and keep them firm, pack with splinters.

Next, set another chunk on top. Not so big
or long this time, and repeat this pattern,
building all the time up and wide, higher
and out till you've got a staggered shape
knitted together with through-stones
bridging front to back. And remember,

to prevent rocking you need to pack
with chocks of stone-shards – they call it
batter. (Strange term, that.) The top level,
the one you finish with, is known as coping.

(A more fitting word you might think.
But that's stonewalling for you. No. Don't

smirk - though I know there could be a joke
in that.) But seriously, once started
it won't be long before you're a dab-hand
at it, and it dawns that if you can manage
to cope you can build yourself a world
without any fear you might get stoned.

The Plantsman, Robert Fortune (1812-1880), considers Rhododendrons

He couldn't help but picture their flowers
as Rococo ornamentation
and a bit over-the-top at that
or, better still, replicas of his wife's newfound dessert
back at home - Jane's piled high *Charlotte Russe*.

And, for sure, their leaves reddening
in the late September sun and hanging abjectly
reminded him of dog-wet tongues;
and their roots, branches, limbs -
smooth, creamwhite - like bone.
Imagine, growing bone.

So trekking the Yangtze river banks,
his sedan chair decked to overflowing
with precious specimens,
he was convinced they leaned after him.
Began to anticipate they'd be waiting in ambush
around each corner, each bend.
Swore he could hear their breathing,
their lifting to turn, their footfall.

So wasn't in the littlest bit surprised
when he heard how they squealed
as he peeled back their leaves, and saw
how they wept as blossom after blossom fell –
soundlessly, slowly, softly -
and knew he needed to give them a home
back home in England.

So travelled hopefully for months
that once they'd arrived in Kew
being so different from his wife's
expected just desserts,
they'd sell like hot cakes.
The rest could go to blazes.

The Gentry Weed: Rhododendrons

For much of the year,
they foster that post-war public-utility look,
that town-council green.
                              Like privet
it's only drizzle's benediction
that lends them a softness, a lightness
so most of the time,
their shield-leaves clack and squeak
as, forcing you to squeeze past,
they outstare you with that bland
non-understanding of Nepalese children
as if it's you that's trespassing,
you that's lost the password.

Till in mid-May, they let
the littlest hints of Summer
go to their heads
in ambushes of vulgar publicness
with colours that smart your eyes,
and a scent so heavy
you're almost tempted to spread it.

It's then you sense a lifting, a rising,
like clouds upon clouds,
their frothy topknots a flouncy bounce
of thousands of Queen Mum Summer hats
charming their own garden parties

or Whitsun brides
smiling their share of the limelight
before shading silently away
to the edges of things.

Japanese Maple, Acer palmatum *"Rubrum"*

A fine October morning – one of those
sky-clear-as-gin days, the sun full but watery
with warmth still in it, midges yo-yoing
over the willow-pattern pool mirroring
its bridge's vermilion and turquoise,
where carp and orf glide silently
through submarine gloom, destination the steps.

And you look up – and it's there, this acer,
as if it's shifted nearer to your view - its wall –
or rather fountain - of leaf (impossible
to describe precisely, you haven't the means,
like when counting its hundreds of leaves and
running out of numbers) - and its colour – such
a palette of crimsons tipped with scarlet where
the light seeps through, or veined with maroons –
that rich texture that wears the sheen of fresh blood –
a burgundy sleekiness capturing refracted light,
making it coppery-metallic in its glistening clarity
like ruby Bohemian glass –

and you concentrate on one leaf –
pull it closely into focus, trying to do justice
to its spreadeagled presence – capture its grandeur
exactly – this stark richness, this garnet with sunlight
streaming through it – and it's so humbly-beautiful,
this one among myriads, this living gem

and suddenly, your gaze shifts to the gravel path
where lying – islanded, sad – is just another
fallen leaf, five-spanned like a road-flattened toad –
lifeless, dried, its beauty gone to ground.

Laburnum's Fragile Affinity

In Winter, pretends to let you inspect
its innernesses: those arcing, arching limbs
whose palpy sapwood you can snap – so -
in your hands; yet its dark-chocolate hardwood
is that hard it mangles machetes, axes.

And in late Spring is garlanded
in superfluities of chains of golden rain
draping their fragrance so readily-sweet
it goes straight to your head, and can sweep you
off your feet – and seriously.
This beauty of bloom is venomous.

But nothing compared
to those peascod pods hanging blandly
and fattening under Summer suns
in bundles the pea-green of mangetout
that tempt you to stretch till your fingers
riffle and split its veritable wealths,
its mayhem.

Come Autumn, leaves bleached sallow
with energies leaching back to its root,
it's a menace of skeletal necklaces – hasbeens,
perhapses - their flaking scales clacking
in the wind and pitted with the bullet grit
of seed the blacks of ebony that can kill.

Aah, suffer the little children …

Pure paradox,
this fragile affinity.

Fishy Triptych

I   Silent, the fish, gliding darkly
to surface by the steps – a pool
within a pool - nudging,
and shoving – circling, and turning –
minds set on outsnapping others
at chance offerings.

Have mouths gawping
like some Charles Laughton movie
with the sound-track turned off –
so blather soundlessly as they trawl the water,
their eyes fixed on arrivals,
looking, and looking -
never letting you off the hook.

II   With hints of lemon, edged in black
the golden orf's scalation -
cross between Anglo-Saxon chainmail
and Klimt's gilded filigree –
is a soft-yellow 22-carat gold offering,
reminiscent of the replica
of the world's biggest nugget
James Bateman once displayed.

III   And the black, fat carp
big as a pig-iron bar –
not really black, but that bilberried
grey-purple-blue of unwashed coal –
the stuff crusted in coal-dust –
with dropped, barbled lips
and baubled eyes that stare straight
through you, as if they know
just how long things have been going on.

Crossing A Young River at Water's Edge

Not the broad swathe and sweep
of Severn, Thames, Humber –
          those fat old ladies of rivers lounging out
          on banksides, surfaces sheening oilily
          under glimmerings of morning sun,
          or that late afternoon veneer
          of reflected light,
          or even that hazy
          dusk-dropping lethargy –
not these

But this newborn thing of a river
that has barely left its bubbling source
lost deep in the deeping countryside
and weaving its undercurrents
in a very jubilation,
          all bounding and bounce,
          rough and tumbling, sploshing around rock
          and outcrop, wheel-circling in pursuit
          of its own being, chasing through glass-clear
          pools, losing self in its own mirrors between sedges
          and kingcup, and wallowing in the whole cram and crush,
          the rush of it, its sloppings and song

So, if you'd only dare, how do you tackle it,
aware it might pull, might even snatch as crossing rock,
toeing foothold, feet teasing, and testing the wetness
and remembering its untamedness,
its unpredictability not yet mastered

And, yes, you take heart, knowing above all else
it is manageable

So go for it,
hedge those bets

extend that hand

lean out for the bankside's haven

Pond Talk

Whoever it was that planned this garden
knows just how to make more than meets the eye.

Two steps rise to a path; the path to a pond
that lends the garden depth – a sense of perspective
so that your gaze first fixes on it
then to the sumach just beyond
and doesn't notice how close the perimeter fence
actually is.

That eye, lying in the grass, drags attention.

Listen, what does this pond say?

> I am here. See me.
> I can accommodate your length in my five feet deeps.
> I move with you as you move.
> I have caught the sky in my eye.
> I am opulent.
> I am full of gold.
> There's no edge on me.

Now, in the Autumn,
under the sumach's antlers turning reddy-gold
the pond seems to be fuller.

Is it leaf or fish, lying in the wet,
lying locked in weed?

Fish! – hanging in still constellations
or darting like falling stars.

And on a clear night
darkness reaffirming the limits of space
and giving the galaxy perspective -
stars shining like fish -
the pond is suddenly bigger
over and above us, all around

and we are drowning in insignificance.

Eel Song

*for Peter Carter, the last eel-trapper of Outwell, Cambridgeshire,
his wife, Sian, and daughter, Rhianna*

I: Life Cycle

Intriguing, this legless land-swimmer that crosses
wet grasses overnight, and crawls up walls.
So unknown is its spawning that country-folk
once thought eels sprung from fallen horse-hair.

No way, though, would you say they were handsome
with that flat moccasin face, all lip and Robert Mitchum
chinless, somehow greasy and sleazy-eyed
as if fazed in amazement of self.

Hatching in trillions of filaments like transparent
ribboning four thousand miles away
in the seaweedy heave of the Saragossa Sea,
they begin their three year wriggle-swim eastwards,

driven by instinct and the Gulf Stream to arrive
in Ireland, needle-thin elvers entering November
estuaries, where lingering till Spring invasions
of English rivers, lagoons and fens. At four years

they're silvering. So long as they steer clear of kiddles,
grigs, putcheons, bucks, fyke nets, hives and eel-pots
can stay two or three decades to reach nearly a metre,
when, without warning, return to spawning beginnings.

II: Weaving the Eel-Pot

It's a stub of a handle to a short blade that
Peter's using – his granddad's – closely held
to body as splicing through the osier-braid,
and running the steel edge speedily down
to split in three, but, stopping short, forming
a stocky wedge where triple strands fan out
their two-foot wands balletic into air.

Repeating this, he pleats one stub-end within
the other, then, ledging it firmly on his knee,
begins weaving the wicker twigs – in, out, in –
between these six willow ribs till makes it into
bottle-shape, funnelled to opening-cheale from
which the caught eel has little chance of escape.
Such is this trapper's take on history's ritual:
like his catch, knows no turning back.

III: Mrs Eelman

- she's Sian. Works in the local P O,
and is glad to, since the six month trapping ban
while eel-stocks pile up, if ever, again.

Remembers a time when each Fenland village
had a handful of trappers; now husband Peter's the last
in this region. Smiles at the tales he's regaled

of family-trading surviving nigh on five hundred
years, with eels as "Fen-gold" bartered for food
and fuel, taxes cashed in eels, even Ely cathedral

built on currency of eel. She knows, though, it's no go
handing down eel-pots to Rhianna, their daughter.
Teenager, she'd never row boats out at dusk to lay

baited traps, or wake early to garner slippery harvests:
hers is a world of make-up, reggae and lads. So, there's
nothing left but being thankful Peter has his punt-gun:

plenty of wild fowl and game for them to live on.
But worries herself silly thinking how he'll pull through
without willow-slips to trigger his fingers alive.

Me, My Mum and the Great Crested Newt

Plucked clear of his wet-quick element,
what fascinated me was his landlubber
slowness, that bland foetus smile, and
his silences - save that zizzing kiss
become wet squelch when I'd held him
between finger and thumb. And pressed.
Just once - for fun - while Mum winced.

But all this was second best to that crested
crenellation which wouldn't/couldn't cut
yet looked dragonish as if to scare off folks,
declaring *Don't you dare touch, don't dare.*
Yet did, zipping my fingers down his spine.

Even Mum couldn't resist that underbelly
ruddiness the colour of meat-rinsed blood,
the olive-black atolls blotching down his
back, and the babypink of spreading hands
and toes plotting out the slow progress
of this toy dinosaur I'd trophied home.

Recalling she'd warned *Isn't yours for keeps,*
I reckoned that no matter how I rigged out
her backyard tub, topping it up with liquorice hose,
plopping pondweed in and teasing out its flagging
fronds, she'd known all along that he'd go sad
and stiff on us: left hanging, dulled, rubbery,
colours drained away, and floating, belly down,
still smiling till I'd flushed him right away,
another stillborn child. How then she cried.

Cupping hands

.... is the way to scoop tiddlers up
flip-flapping their inching quickness
in your palms. But don't pick minnows:
their sliding green's so dull. And, anyway,
pin-thin and darting, they're difficult to fish:
know how to hide in bankside shallows.
No, go for the stickleback, especially
the male - gem of a fellow with his ruddy
tummy, his marbled flank and back,
his eyes wide as silences. But mind
that trio of spines.

Aged eight, I jam-jarred one from the copse
(the chirring burn, its rills, its froth - birches
spritting – angled bracken - and blackbirds
working their everywhere song) took him
with weed to our backyard and its Staffordshire
blue-black brick, its ivy spidering the wall.

Once decanted into Mum's enamelled bath
with the daily-changed water, we watched
his turns, his back-pedalling, his hanging still.

Five days on he gave me my first touch
of death in Mum's cupped hands, his gaze
away, body stiff, while hers heaved and stirred,
the tears silently sliding down her cheeks.

Years later learned about her stillbirth:
the lidded eyes, the wide-splayed hands.

Small Fry

for Mary, for Rob

Remember Rob telling how, as a lad,
his cupped hands worked the water,
his angled palms pushing back towards
the bankside and skirting around pebbles,
little finger trailing the gravel in a silent glide –
steady, steady – against the brook's lulling
push downstream, its surface mirrored in glimmers
of sunlight like fractured glass,
the water feet-deep, gin-clear, and those splinters
of minnows, darting this way, that or hanging still –
tail, fin, pectorals on hold, gills pulsing – and, scoop,
he swished them up, and out, time after time,
their grey-green leanness flick-flacking in his hand,
their pin-eyes a panic, head flapping, mouth
gawping till he slipped them into that jamjar world
of chickweed, their circling swirls transforming
to an easing freedom of sorts – Remember this?

He wouldn't have dreamt of making a meal
of them. And yet no second questioning
his request for whitebait: each piled fish
a masterpiece of reticulated scale – such
frail armature – lambent and shading through
silver to white to grey, the dark targets of their eyes
passively accusing in silent negations of all
they had been, their life to come, their everything,
taken away too soon. What a world to feast
his wishes on, little thinking how within a month
the morphine would kick in, his mouth turning
to gawp, his eyes glaring that gone-away stare
of panic and acceptance, his hands cupped
to capture nothings, and letting everything
slide away, freed at last.

Elemental

I: Earth, the inheritor

Beneath feet.
Always.

Take dust in the Garden
palmed to cupped handful,
balled into clay,
rolled, moulded,
squidged, thumbed up,
then blessed
by heavenly breath,

and - swish –
rising to Adam:
genesis of mankind's woe.

For us, his snaking away
with Paradise
is only regained when,
wide-mouthed – awed, appalled
and intoning ashes to ashes,
dust to dust -
earth admits
every damned thing.

II: *Air, the sharer*

Free Air the garage forecourt exhorts.

But thoughts of dis-owning it
never threaten our lips.

Besides which
releasing what's keeping
body and soul together
isn't much of a wheeze.

III: *Fire, the inspirer*

Hot stuff, this:
warm-hearted mover
and nimble dancer.

Greedy blighter, too:
devours everything
it lights on.

Resourceful trail-blazer:
allows no obstacle;
clears ground in seconds.

Scion of Hell:
meeting its match in Lucifer
springs into life.

Is God's other toy.

Ask Prometheus …

IV: Water, the guarantor

Of blood: slippage of limbs' rhythmic river
              that keeps pulse-tick going, its plasma-pact
              clotting bruise to damson. Knows it cannot
              atrophy. Needs to dance. To sing.

Of sweat: everywhere, from head to foot,
              signal of illness: beading fevered brow;
              and tracking shivering back.
              Or work-time's manifesto
              underwriting armpit
              and crotch, breeding at omphalos ring
              and nosing between toes.

Of tears: always close to home, from birth-slap
              through to wedding ceremony, and chief mourner.
              At other times, salt of the earth;
              sibling of mucous and snot.
              Wiped out by rag, hanky or back of hand.

Listen to it
              sizzling in the crem's incinerator,

              running to the last.